CERAMIC PAINTING

Project Book

Learn how to create a
collection of ceramic painting.

5 projects inside!

INTRODUCTION

Welcome to the wonderful world of Ceramic Painting!

Learning a new skill is always exciting – we're here to help you get started. Ceramic painting is a great way to explore and experiment with your paints - being as simple or as adventurous as you like. You can start with just a small paintbrush and a couple of colours, or add a variation of colours and some stencils to create some intricate designs.

The finished designs can either be sealed with a glaze varnish, or left as a matte finish. Much will depend on what you want to use it for afterwards. For example; if you paint a mug that you wish to drink out of, it needs to be sealed with a glaze. Ceramic sealants are very inexpensive and can be bought from most art suppliers.

Ceramic painting can be a very therapeutic skill to learn on your own, or it can bring a group of people together. It's also a fantastic activity for kids to do throughout their school holidays, or a birthday party idea. Why not fill a room with different ceramic objects and see what creations they come up with?

This kit provides everything you need to make your first piece of art, which means getting started is easy. We have included four other projects within this book to help you along the way. Just like any new skill, ceramic painting may be a little tricky at first. Experiment with different colours and techniques. But most importantly, enjoy yourself.

Let's get started on your ceramic painting journey.

Top Tip – Before starting any craft with paint, make sure to cover your work surface with an easy to wipe mat, or some old pieces of newspaper to protect your surfaces!

KIT CONTENTS

WHAT'S INCLUDED:

· 3x Acrylic paints
· 3x Ceramic trinket dishes
· Small paintbrush

YOU'LL NEED:

· Toothpick, skewers or plastic spoons
· Sponges (assorted sizes and shapes)
· Scrapers
· Masking tape
· Paintbrushes (assorted sizes and shapes)
· A drying rack
· Varnish
· Some kitchen roll or a wet cloth to wipe any
  excess paint.

Ingredients:
Poly (Acrylic Acid), Calcium Carbonate, 1, 3-Pentanedoil, 2, 2, 4-Trimethyl-, Monoisobutyrate, Water. Pigment
Yellow 14, Pigment Green 8, Titanium Oxide and Pigment Violet 23.

THE BASICS

To get started, all you need is some acrylic paints (as little or as many as you like) and some ceramic to paint on. If you are a beginner, it's a good idea to start off by painting on a smooth, flat surface to really engage and get into the flow of how to paint on your ceramic.

We recommend starting off with a medium sized paintbrush. If you are painting on a larger scale surface and want to paint all over, then a wider, flatter shaped paintbrush is more suitable. The bigger your paintbrush, the smoother your brush strokes will be to cover the surface. A smaller paintbrush on larger surfaces will require more strokes, meaning the overall finish may be slightly patchy or uneven. Keep your thinner, more defined paintbrushes, for the delicate details you want to add throughout or at the end for decoration.

We would always recommend using acrylic paint for painting on ceramic. Acrylic paint is incredibly versatile and can be applied to ceramic without it having to go into a kiln to be fired. Whilst durable and not too runny, acrylic paint is also easier to blend. Be aware, however, that acrylic paint drys quite quickly - if you want to blend your colours, you will have to work efficiently! If you don't have acrylic paint, you can also use oil paints, enamel paints or any water-based paints.

Your ceramic painting will dry with a matte finish. If you prefer a glossy finished look, you can use a clear water-based ceramic varnish to create this glazed effect. This will also lock in the acrylic paint and prevent it from cracking.

BLOCK COLOUR PAINTING:

This is a very easy, simple and neat way to create abstract shapes using masking tape and acrylic paint. Making sure your surface is clean and dust free, cut your lengths of masking tape and lay them down on your ceramic where you do not want the paint to be transferred to. Paint on the uncovered parts of your ceramic. When you are finished, peel it back to reveal your design!

PAINTING WITH PALETTE KNIVES:

Painting with a palette knife is a great way to spread and move your paint with a tool other than a paintbrush. Acrylic paint is a great medium to use for this technique. It's thick enough to be spread and create movement, without being too runny. Load your paint onto your palette knife and, using the long straight edges, sweep across your surface. This will blend your colours together (if using two) and create texture on your surface.

SPONGE PAINTING:

Sponge painting is probably one of the easiest and quickest ways of painting on ceramic. All you need is a couple of clean, dry sponges and the paint colours you want to use. Using sponges on your surface can sometimes enable you to create softer looking finishes, rather than the harsher brush strokes that you might find with a paintbrush. You can blend your colours very easily and create a beautiful ombré effect with your paint.

STENCIL PAINTING:

Stencil painting is a technique used to create designs repetitively by transferring paint over holes/cut out shapes onto the chosen surface. You can do this by either using a paintbrush or a sponge. Most of the time, you will have to go over this more than once to give your paint a second coat and make sure it has fully transferred. Once your paint has transferred and dried, you will need to be super careful to gently lift up your stencil and reveal your paint design.

Top Tip – When choosing your ceramic to paint, we would recommend painting on unglazed ceramic as acrylic paints struggle to lay correctly on top. This could lead to your paint being vulnerable to scratching off your ceramic if it is glazed prior to painting.

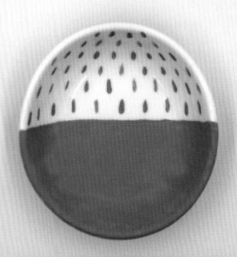

WARNINGS!

All the makes included in this book are designed specifically for adults.

Keep all ingredients and finished products out of the reach of children.

Some ingredients may irritate; always avoid contact with skin and eyes. If ingredients come into contact with eyes or skin, wash with water immediately.

Do not ingest; if accidentally ingested drink water and seek medical advice.

We recommend wearing old clothes or overalls when partaking in creative activities. Cover work surfaces to avoid mess.

TRINKET
DISHES

10

TRINKET DISHES

Both beautiful and useful. Perfect to keep jewellery safe, never lose your favourite earrings or rings again! These beautiful trinket dishes are perfect to keep jewellery safe, or as a unique gift to your loved ones.

KIT INCLUDES
· 3x Acrylic paints
· 3x Ceramic trinket dishes
· Small paintbrush

METHOD

1. Make sure your work surface is covered with an easy to wipe mat or cloth, then gather all your contents together.

2. Use your brush to gently draw a straight line down the middle of your trinket. This will be your partition where you will paint one side, and decorate the other.

3. Use the finer end of your paintbrush to accentuate your line and start to fill in the right side of your trinket with colour. Keep going until you have completely filled the entire half.

4. Repeat this process for all three trinkets. Make sure to clean your brush in between each one. Now, take a wet cloth or piece of kitchen roll and wipe around the side of your trinkets, removing any excess paint.

5. To decorate, start to add your detail by gently dotting the colour with your paintbrush. You can do this by adding polka dots, lines, or if you feel really adventurous, why not try some swirls with your brush?

6. Once you have repeated this process on all three of your trinkets, leave them to dry for 24hrs on a clean, flat surface.

NOTES

Use the space below to make your own personal notes on the previous project to help when you come back to make it again!

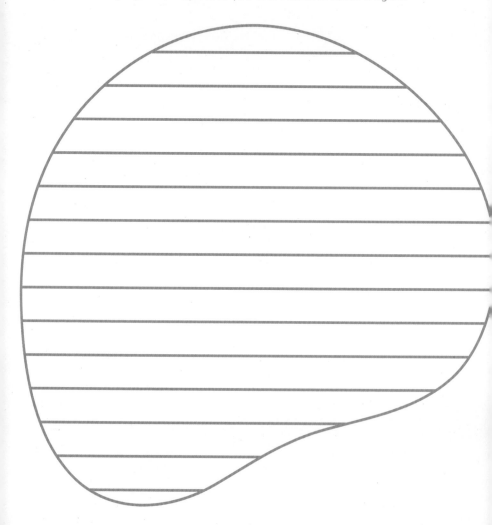

SUNSET FRAME

SUNSET FRAME

Get into a summer mood with this tropical sunset inspired frame!
Use a sponge to help blend and create this fabulous gradient
effect.

WHAT YOU WILL NEED

- 6x Acrylic paints
- 2x Clean sponges
- Masking tape
- Paper napkin
- Ceramic Frame

METHOD

1. Cover the inside of your photo frame with masking tape so that your paint does not accidentally blend onto the photo part of your frame.

2. Now, gather your paints and tools together. We recommend using two clean sponges and a paper napkin for dabbing. The colours we have chosen are variants of shades, as we are going to show you how to do a sponge gradient effect.

3. Transfer a very small amount of your lightest colour onto your dabbing paper. Now, mix with an even smaller amount of your second lightest colour. Dab away at this on the paper until you have blended the colours together.

4. Using your sponge, begin dabbing the paint onto the top of your ceramic frame. When you have covered a good amount, slightly take the pressure off and then start with your next colour. Make sure to blend the two colours together so they flow effortlessly.

5. Continue step 3 and 4 as you work your way through your colours, making sure to leave enough room as you are going down to finish with your darkest colour at the bottom. Depending on the vibrancy of the colours, you may need to add a little bit of white paint to soften the colours as you blend them together.

6. Leave your photo frame lying flat for 24hrs to dry fully. Once dry, stand upright and take away the masking tape to reveal a clean space to pop your photo in.

NOTES

Use the space below to make your own personal notes on the previous project to help when you come back to make it again!

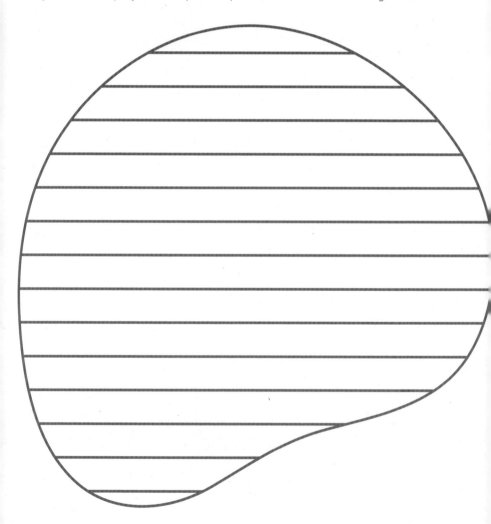

COASTERS

COASTERS

Create some colourful coasters! These coasters are hand painted using palette knives, creating a texture that is completely unique. Perfect for any occasion and will bring a splash of colour to your own home.

WHAT YOU WILL NEED

- 2x Palette knives
- 4x Acrylic paints
- Ceramic coasters

METHOD

1. Gather all your contents together for your palette painting. For this, you will need 2 palette knives and 3 colours, as well as your white base paint. Start by painting the base of your coaster white.

2. Leave your coaster to dry for around 12hrs to make sure the white paint has completely dried and is ready to be painted on. Next, squeeze a blob or two of your colours onto your palette knife. Using the flat edge of your knife, sweep across your surface.

3. Move the paint in different directions around your coaster using the knife. You will notice your paint will start to blend into one another and also, potentially create a new colour. Here, our blue and yellow has started to create a lovely medium colour of green.

4. You can then add a third colour. Continue to move your palette knife around your coaster in whichever way you choose. You will create a lovely, textured surface as your paint continues to dry.

5. When you are happy with your chosen colours, lightly dab the pointed part of your other palette knife on top of the paint. Make sure every part of your coaster is covered.

6. Leave your coaster to dry for 24 – 48hrs this time. The paint will be slightly thicker and will need a little bit longer to set.

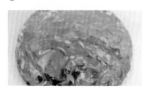

NOTES

Use the space below to make your own personal notes on the previous project to help when you come back to make it again!

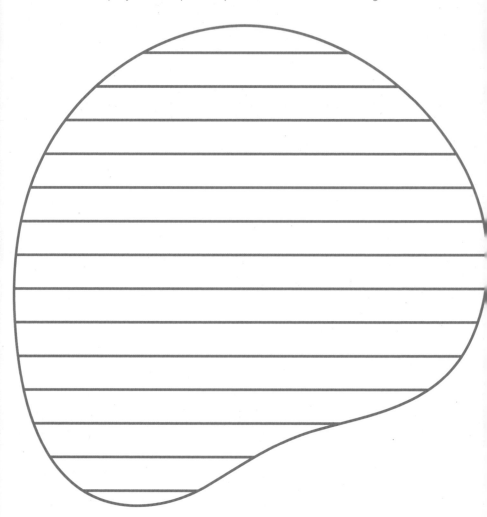

FLORAL HANGING

FLORAL HANGING

Perfect for hanging on a wall, this round ceramic decoration features a colourful, hand-painted floral design. Using a combination of masking tape and a stencil to get the best structure out of your painted petal shape.

WHAT YOU WILL NEED

· Small paintbrush
· Flower stencil
· Masking tape
· 4x Acrylic paints
· Cocktail stick
· Varnish
· Ceramic decoration
· Ribbon

METHOD

1. For this make, we are going to paint over a stencil on a round ceramic decoration with a pre-cut hole. Before you start, pop some masking tape around the edges of your decoration to create that neat painted edge. Now, you can begin painting in the base colour. We have chosen black, but you can choose whichever colour you wish as long as your paint will show up on top.

2. Leave your base coat to dry for 24hrs. Once dry, lay your stencil and secure the edges down with some masking tape to keep it in place.

3. Start to paint your petals in whichever design you wish. Be careful not to go outside the lines on the tops of the petals. Go over the petals 2-3 times to ensure no undercoat is showing through.

4. Leave the paint to dry for a couple of hours. Remove the masking tape and slowly start to peel away your stencil revealing the pattern underneath. Now you can remove the masking tape from around the side of your decoration.

5. You can leave your painting how it is, or if you would like to add an extra design on there, grab yourself a cocktail stick and add some little dots onto your petals. We have decorated all the blue petals.

6. Once you are happy with your extra design elements, leave your decoration to dry for 24hrs. If you want a glossy effect, you will need to add a clear water-based ceramic varnish which you can buy in most art stores.

7. Once your wall hanging is fully dry, you can loop and tie your ribbon through the hole in the top of the ceramic decoration.

NOTES

Use the space below to make your own personal notes on the previous project to help when you come back to make it again!

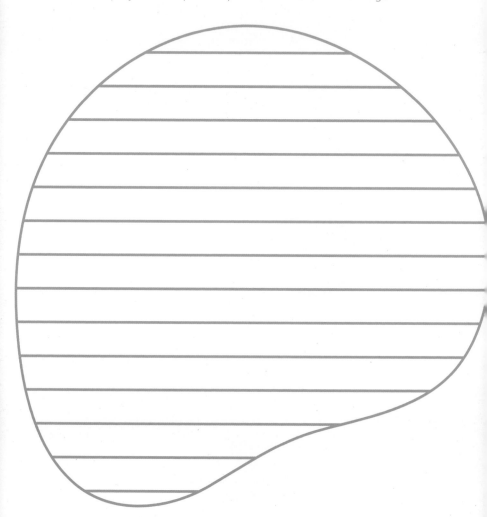

JEWELLERY BOX

JEWELLERY BOX

Keep trinkets and treasures safely stored away with this beautifully hand painted jewellery box. Painted using masking tape to help create these structured stripes. Great to add a modern twist into your home décor!

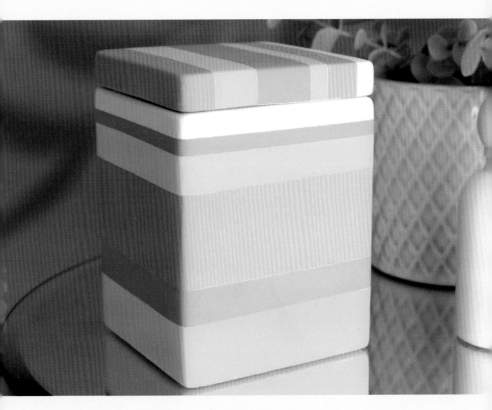

WHAT YOU WILL NEED

· Small paintbrush
· Masking tape
· 3x Acrylic paints
· Ceramic box

METHOD

1. Take out all the contents needed for this make. We recommend using 3 different colours. We're going to do a block effect painting - this works well if the colours are slightly different from one another. You will also need some masking tape for this one!

2. Stick your masking tape along the top and sides of your box where you do not want the paint to go. Try to keep it very straight. The masking tape will hold your paint in place and keep nice straight lines on the parts you have painted. When you come to remove it, you will have very neat edges.

3. Use your first colour to paint all the sections you want to do with this one. While it is drying, you can move onto your next colour. Don't forget to also pop some masking tape along the bottom of your box as this will all add to that extra neat finish!

4. You may need to remove some masking tape from the very first part you painted, and re-position it to paint the section next to it. Once you have done all your colours, leave to dry and then repeat this process again, making sure there are two coats of paint on your box.

5. Leave your box to dry for 24hrs. When it is dry to the touch, you can start to remove your masking tape. Do this process very slowly and very gently. This will make sure you do not take up any paint when removing the tape.

6. And there is your box! Remember, you will have masking tape on the bottom of your box which will need removing! If you want a glossy effect, you will need to add a clear water-based ceramic varnish which you can buy in most art stores.